REFLECTIONS

DOUG HELM

REFLECTIONS

Looking Back on Life

Fresno, CA

Copyright © 2021, Doug Helm

All rights reserved. No part of this book may be used or reproduced by any means, graphic, electronic, or mechanical (including any information storage retrieval system) without the express written permission from the author, except in the case of brief quotations for use in articles and reviews wherein appropriate attribution of the source is made.

Published in the United States by Ignite Press.
ignitepress.us

ISBN: 978-1-953655-34-9 (Amazon Print)
ISBN: 978-1-953655-35-6 (IngramSpark) PAPERBACK
ISBN: 978-1-953655-36-3 (IngramSpark) HARDCOVER
ISBN: 978-1-953655-37-0 (E-book)

To reach the author, send a message to:
reflectionsbydoughelm@gmail.com

Because of the dynamic nature of the Internet, web addresses or links contained in this book may have been changed since publication and may no longer be valid. The content of this book and all expressed opinions are those of the author and do not reflect the publisher or the publishing team. The author is solely responsible for all content included herein.

Library of Congress Control Number: 2020924317

Cover design by Salman Sarwar
Edited by Andrew Hirst
Interior design by Michelle M. White

I dedicate this book to my father, Jack Helm.

Dad wrote his reflections daily in a journal throughout his adult life and encouraged me to do the same.

In writing this book of reflections I was inspired by his encouragement.

It is one of the many pieces of advice he gave me over the years which have made me a better person.

Acknowledgements

To the people in my life who have inspired me in writing these reflections:

To my wife, Anne, who is the love of my life and who encouraged me to write these reflections in a journal;

To my parents, Jane and Jack Helm, who were the source of so many examples and so much love, despite ours being a normal family with imperfections;

To my sisters and brothers, Jane, John, Ted, Lucy and David, who I love and have learned from while growing up and continuing in adulthood;

To my Grandmother, Mayme Schulten, who has been the most loving example in my life;

To my children, Kim, Amy, Douglas, Meghan and Todd, for my many loving experiences with them and for the joy and privilege of being their father;

To my stepchildren, Erin, Adam, and especially Taylor, who came into my life unexpectedly and gives me joy;

To Larry Mattingly, who taught me so much about quietly making a difference in the world;

DOUG HELM

To my grandchildren, who have expanded my ability to love, give and enjoy;

And to a universe of wonderful things which surround us every day.

Table of Contents

Introduction *1*

Racial Tension Moments *3*

Pandemic Thoughts *5*

A Chance to Be More *7*

A Few Gifts *9*

An Opportunity *10*

Amy *11*

Simplicity *13*

Anne *14*

Cars *16*

Crookedness *18*

Dad *19*

Douglas *21*

Difficulties *23*

Blinking Life   24

Fatherly Advice   26

Friends Walking   27

Chair   29

Gratefulness   30

Beauty Unexpected   32

Experiences   33

Impact of a Friend   34

Being More   36

Meaning   38

Mom   40

Memories of Children When they were Young   42

Kim   43

Life Realized   45

Meghan   46

Mistakes   48

Countless Blessings   49

Lincoln   51

Nature   53

Sam   54

Sixty   55

Singing   56

Swimming   57

Sisters and Brothers   59

Youth Memories   61

Struggle   63

Taylor   64

Growing Pains   66

Moving Sunrise   67

Giving Back   68

Todd   69

Visiting Grandchildren   70

Elderly Beauty   72

The Most Beautiful Thing   74

Wheat Thins and Muenster Cheese   76

When I See Myself   78

Woman in Church   80

Young Children Singing   81

Larry 82

Making a Cake 83

Gifts from Children 85

Louisville Orchestra Pops 87

Beach Vacation 88

Turning Seventy 89

Teets Court 90

Riding the Bus 92

Looking Around 94

Untitled Quote 95

January Thoughts 96

Illusions 97

Conclusion 99

About the Author 103

*"Wisdom is knowing I am nothing.
Love is knowing I am everything.
And in between the two my life moves."*

Nisargadatta Maharaj

Introduction

I had never been one to write down personal experiences in my adult life. I was busy raising kids, taking care of a home and growing my career. If I wrote anything, it involved work or related continuing education.

As life began to slow in recent years, I have had more time to look back and reflect.

In 2006, on a family vacation, while walking on the beach, the many present experiences were vivid in my mind and I wanted to record them.

The next day, I took a paper and pen on a walk and, when I got to a secluded place on the beach, I sat down and wrote a short reflection.

My wife gave me a journal shortly thereafter, and suggested using it to record more reflections.

Over the 15 years since then, as reflections have come to me, I have added them to my journal. Reflections were written from my heart as thoughts came to me, and usually in a very few minutes.

As I gathered more reflections, I saw that they summed up my life in areas important to me: personal relationships, nature, faith, people I have helped and who have helped me, and growth from good experiences and in struggles. I thought more about sharing them with people important to me.

I could have just left the journal among my things, to be discovered eventually. But some may not see them. Most would not be able to read my terrible penmanship! And some may want to discuss them with me while I am still alive. Or the journal may be misplaced and never be seen.

A friend writing a book made me think of doing a book myself. I began to explore that possibility.

I tried to talk myself out of doing this: should I take the risk of sharing such deeply personal experiences? Do I really have something important enough to share? Aren't books just for the famous, which I am not?

Eventually, the risk of not writing a book overrode the risks of regret, vulnerability and not allowing others who may read it to make up their own minds about what I have written.

I humbly offer this resulting book of reflections to you as part of the simple life I have lived.

If it touches you in some way, I am grateful.

Racial Tension Moments

The uncertainty of things is disturbing and unsettling;

Issues of safety, fairness, peacefulness, racial equality –

All are questioned and debated.

It causes pain and hurt.

Injustice exists.

How do we change that?

How can there be more listening, compassion, caring?

What are the best ways to lessen the pain?

How do we assure accountability for unjust actions?

What does an individual, a family, a neighborhood, a workplace do?

How can we soothe wounds?

How do people with no answers find them?

When is it my job and not someone else's to change?

I just know it causes me to question, want the pain to stop, ache for those in helpless positions,

And want things to be safe and peaceful.

Prayer is nice, but doing, listening, caring with actions is nicer.

Pandemic Thoughts

As I wake up at home, I connect differently. So many things part of my ritual are not within reach.

At first, denial. This can't be. It will change. I can go on with my regular life.

But gradually, I face that I can't. I am home facing silence and stillness. Scared, anxious. Wondering how I will handle it. Enough food? Will I catch it? Can I sit still? Shocked by the news and possibilities. How long will it last?

Days seem long. Waiting to end and sleep. Waking to the same. Relying on others for help. Everything I do makes me question. Where is God in all of this? Am I six feet away? Did I wash my hands after that?

Changing habits to adjust: work at home, read online, setting new rituals. Creating a new flow: Getting dressed, creating a workstation. New exercise regimes; eating less. Keeping my workspace clean.

I face the fact it is not just me. I look for ways to connect with family. Phone calls. Facetime; sending and receiving pictures of experiences. Becoming aware of how the world is responding. Many with horrible experiences worse than mine and making it. Encouraging words on social media. So many sacrifices!

Simplicity returning! Smiling and waving to others on walks. Appreciating nature. Smells, sounds, sights, adjusting to new realities as they slowly emerge. Memories of youth, when some of this was normal flow I lived with. Less importance of non-essentials.

Rekindling hope for the unknown; not knowing how long, forever impact, what permanently changes. Beginning to live with what tomorrow brings.

Can I be happier for this moment? Can I keep on adjusting? What will be my new way of living? Resisting waiting for the old normal to return. Not knowing what new normal will be.

Accepting what I don't control. Seeing examples of others settling into the new now. Seeing them appreciate those around them and what is. Doing their part to help. Seeing old problems as less important.

Embracing this moment. Accepting ups and downs. Wanting to have more hope and to be better at letting go.

Laughing at myself. Singing to myself. Viewing what my life has been so far. Allowing new thoughts to sneak into my head.

Wanting just to be contented with the moment and what I can do to be nice.

Being Thankful.

A Chance to Be More

Very few have a second chance.

I was lucky;

To have an unexpected meeting;

To experience someone special;

To begin to talk

And have things in common;

To gradually become friends,

And just be there for a while with each other,

Eventually sharing the hurt

And seeing specialness and beauty;

Beginning to trust and be trusted;

To laugh and be childlike again;

To share mutual experiences;

To fall in love and marry;

To grow with and learn from;

To develop new traditions with;

To have the opportunity to grow old with.
And to be grateful.

A Few Gifts

I have a few gifts I have passed on:

To a spouse, unconditional love and loyalty.

To children, loving commitment and example.

To siblings, acceptance, availability, honesty.

To grandchildren, time, simple gifts, answering questions.

To friends, keeping in touch, sharing memories.

To fellow workers, helpfulness, trustworthiness.

To people at church, faith, singing, joining in.

To those with differences, humility, acceptance, hope.

An Opportunity

After years of waiting until tomorrow

For things I will do to get my life straight, so I can begin to enjoy being happy,

I finally realize when these few imperfections are fixed,

More will come.

And some will always be

A revelation and relief;

To feel less pressure

To work on dusting myself off for the day there will be no dust;

And just enjoying this day

For its beauty,

And the opportunity to grow

For the people I can love more,

And learn from more;

For opportunities to laugh, sing and give others a boost.

And tomorrow will bring another such opportunity!

Amy

Dark, beautiful hair

Loving smile

Quietly focused

Profound

Playing sports

Loving circle of friends

Paddle board champion

Tanned and beautiful

Building sandcastles at the beach.

Quizzing her boyfriends –

What does your Father do?

Coed party in the basement

Father-daughter dances

Desert lover

Reader of books

Getting me to read books

Dorm trips

Parent weekends

Galloping run

Pigtails and ponytails

Earplugs

Strong swimming stroke

Independent and free

Touching my heart.

Simplicity

And after your life is over,

You are simply the lives of those you have touched,

And how they are different because of interacting with you.

You are occasional fleeting memories people have for having known you.

You hope it will be more good than bad,

But only time tells.

But while alive –

Aahhhh!

The opportunity to know this and to alter what memories might be someday;

To just relish each moment;

To appreciate the beauty and the wonder of a quick-moving existence;

And to hope to make some difference.

Anne

A good mother, spouse and friend,

You take life on to your soul.

You model goodness, dedication, friendship, loyalty, honesty, trustworthiness.

You make the clothes smell sweet.

You cook with love.

You make wonderful egg sandwiches!

You switch and take the oldest so your girl can have the newest.

You shout, "That's my baby!"

You power shop and buy gifts that show your thoughtfulness.

You stand up and are firm at the difficult moments.

You stay up late to wait and show you care.

You exhaust yourself listening to the innermost of those you love.

You think before you talk.

REFLECTIONS

You reserve your deepest for the most important in your life.

You say, "Move away from me", when you need space.

You feel good in your skin.

You drink wine and laugh.

You rest when you are tired.

You show pain to the few you love dearly.

You give passion and life experiences to your students.

You set steel boundaries.

You refuse to accept indifference and lack of genuineness.

You love this man unconditionally.

You demand every ounce out of life.

And you are my best friend!

Cars

Adding excitement, imagination and markers to growing up

1954 Ford station wagon: lime green three-speed; third seat to fit a family of six; memories of everyday outings and trips; traveling to and from Alaska with three brothers and sisters, to and from my father's Army assignment.

1950s Fords and Chevys, Buicks, Cadillacs; visiting neighborhood car dealer showrooms every fall when the new models were introduced; sitting in different models, taking in the new smells and memorizing every detail; dreaming of owning and driving some day.

1958 Corvette: owned by a young neighbor always working on details; asking him questions as I walked by; him inviting me over to see up close; sitting in the driver's seat and imagining; black with red interior; four-speed convertible; invited on a dream road rally trip with him and his girlfriend; mesmerized by the pick-up in speed, revving of the motor, gear shifting; becoming my dream car for life.

1961 Chevy Bel Air four-door: aqua with white trim; the family's only car; taking for my driver's license test; volunteering for errands just to drive and taking a long way home, often by a girlfriend's house; competing for drive time with parents and a brother and sister on weekends; taking on dates; cruising drive ins with friends; just driving around and listening to the radio.

1965 Chevy Impala convertible; dream car owned by an aunt whose husband was a car salesman and had as a demo; aqua with white interior; working up the courage to ask to borrow for my senior prom and her saying yes; exhilarating drives all day and to the prom with the top down.

1964 Chevy Impala Super Sport; navy blue; bucket seats and console; sporty hubcaps; the thrill and excitement of owning my first car; 30 monthly GMAC payments; countless drives with friends, on dates, to college; washing it every week with the radio on.

Never being able to travel a road, pass a parking lot or car dealership without noticing every car and its features and imagining driving them.

All time markers in a youth of loving cars.

Carrying over the importance in my adult life,

And passing on to a son –

Keeping memories alive!

Crookedness

Some of the people I love are not aligned.

I get moments of peace from accepting it

And my lack of control over it.

Maybe it is God helping me to face not controlling.

I will never fully understand.

Dad

Strong, handsome man,

Taller than life when I was small –

So striking in his Army uniform,

Tying his tie in the mirror when we talked.

His square jaw and crooked nose.

The wonder of assorted things on his dresser.

Throwing the baseball in the driveway.

Struggling in life with goodness forever marbled in.

Asleep in his recliner,

Watching Johnny Carson,

Drinking coffee and eating cheese and crackers.

Singing 'Me And My Shadow' and snapping his fingers.

Getting fruit from Paul's.

His unique G in 'DOUG' on Christmas gifts, giving away he was Santa.

Playing poker and bridge with seriousness.

Conversations in his office over a sandwich,

Being touching and compassionate toward those in need.

Reading books,

Giving me dress hats to wear.

Cleaning toilets with dignity.

Pride in his Mom and Dad

Walking around Seneca Park with him.

Carving the turkey at Thanksgiving.

Mass at the Cathedral together.

Not afraid of death.

Giving away more than he had.

And forever leaving an impression on many others.

Douglas

First son,

Fearless youth.

Becoming tender, gentle, vulnerable.

Holding him through fears and troubles,

Sleeping by the door at night to be near his parents when he was scared.

Handsome.

Loving.

Strong.

Fast bike rides of joy,

Leaning into the sun to get more tanned.

Heartily laughing.

Drinking coffee together in the white house kitchen.

His with creamer he loved

Galloping down the soccer field.

Love of nature and travel.

Passion for experiences on the edge.

Endless basketball in the driveway, being LaBradford Smith.

Forever in my thoughts.

Difficulties

Everything in life is good;

it's just a matter of degrees.

And how I see the opportunity in the midst of difficulties.

I learn much more from my failures than from my successes.

Blinking Life

Eyes open and life begins.

I learn to eat and to walk,

To cry,

To laugh,

To listen,

And then to speak.

I make friends and learn about life.

I grow into adolescence and feel awkward,

And eventually gain confidence and pass that on to others as opportunities arise.

I form meaningful relationships.

I find my talents and develop them.

I find work that is meaningful and contribute.

I marry.

I have children and guide them to independence.

REFLECTIONS

I mellow, learn to enjoy and drink life in.
I learn from my mistakes and grow mature.
I sit and relax.
I work through the pains.
I become an example for others and them for me.
I believe more in a deeper meaning,
And something good beyond us all.

I grow old.
I let others care for me more.
I become quiet.
I have hope and great memories.
I feel the depth of God in a powerful world.
I let go.

Eyes close and life ends.

Fatherly Advice

He was shaving,

Looking in the mirror,

Giving me some advice as I stood nearby,

His eyes glancing at me through the mirror at times,

And me drinking in every word.

He turned and pointed his razor at me to get my attention.

I looked back attentively and respectfully

"All you have to do to be exceptional in this world is to do what is expected of you...

every day!"

Friends Walking

It started with two neighbors seeing each other walking and deciding to walk together sometimes.

It became a Sunday morning thing we did.

Conversations developed,

Simple and distant at first,

Expanding into deeper areas –

Family,

Faith,

Politics.

Making a difference.

The way we each tried to live,

We grew to things in common

And to differences.

Hesitant at first to go beyond the surface,

Touching on things and veering off,

Gradually we introduced difficult areas of our lives;

Pains we had endured;

Ways we each tried to live our faith;

Family members with difficulties;

The enormity of our love for them and attempts to reach out and heal;

Facing the limitations of life.

We developed trust

And introduced layers of things.

Values translating to sensitivity.

Challenging each other through differences,

Getting into, "Why do you do that?"

And, "Why didn't you do this?"

Values always overriding the few ways we differ,

Time and distance began to evaporate with conversational intensity,

And, at the end of a walk, lingering to talk before breaking off and going back to our lives,

Enriched by the experience.

Chair

Give me a chair to read in

By a window where I see the sun,

A place to contemplate the goodness of life,

To think about those I love,

And to forgive others – and even myself.

To relax in,

With a stool to put my feet up on,

To smile and let go in,

And I will be fine.

Gratefulness

I am grateful for:

The ability to laugh at and learn from my mistakes;

How I can enjoy many good things –

Singing,

Talking,

Listening,

Nature.

Personal, meaningful relationships.

Financial security.

The ability to believe in the impossible, the unimaginable and the hard to believe.

Walking in the sun.

How I can say I am sorry when I have hurt,

And forgive when I am hurt.

Enjoying family and good friends.

Reading,

REFLECTIONS

Learning,

Growing,

And loving those who matter.

Beauty Unexpected

I took a turn off a main road on my way to a meeting,

On a winding road

By beautiful scenery.

A meandering creek on the roadside, with a waterfall.

Several country churches with members' cars in adjacent parking lots,

Blue wildflowers on the edge of the road, blowing in the rush of passing cars.

A group of horses in the meadow.

Intermittent curved sections of road with trees overhanging, creating cool shade.

The sun shining off of the pavement.

Long, winding sectional fence, newly whitewashed.

Some stone fences, many years old:

Time to think, relax, and enjoy –

Something wonderful I never would have expected.

Experiences

I have loved a wonderful woman,

Nurtured relationships with children and grandchildren,

Known great friends,

Sung with an orchestra,

Walked beautiful beaches,

Tasted great foods,

Taught others what I know,

And learned from people of all types.

I have laughed, cried and wondered,

Learned from my mistakes,

Forgiven those who have hurt me.

I have seen the power and wonder of God

In a bright and mysterious world,

With more to come!

Impact of a Friend

I read an article by a woman in her 20s who, along with her husband, met with Thomas Merton. They were sharing the husband's graduate school dissertation on Thomas Merton's life.

She was impacted tremendously by Merton, who had related to her in a way that had "illuminated me on how to live".

This made me reflect on the similar way Fr. Lawrence Mattingly had impacted me.

I was in my 20s. Larry was a Franciscan who had spent time with me and my former wife through a common Marriage Encounter experience (interestingly, the woman in the story above was also divorced from her first husband).

Larry allowed us to see his humanity and shortcomings, in addition to his great qualities, and at the same time to see our goodness and the power of living our simple family life.

This, from a person of enormous greatness in terms of impacting others in his Franciscan community, throughout the country and as a missionary in third-world Franciscan communities.

REFLECTIONS

My life was elevated over my time with Larry to a person who believed in his goodness and the impact I could have on the world.

All from a chance encounter.

Being More

I would like to have been more,

As I get to the other side of life,

And look back at most and forward to some.

Could I have made a bigger difference?

Could I have solved more problems?

Could I have left a better legacy?

Been famous?

Cured a disease?

Written a bestselling book?

Maybe.

But I couldn't have smelled the sweetness of life more.

I couldn't have laughed, loved, tasted, experienced things more fully.

And in the end,

I was mostly

REFLECTIONS

A good husband,
A good father,
A good friend.

Meaning

Is meaning in life something I wait for?

Something that will start any minute,

When I get it together,

Work out my problems,

Adjust to the endless tasks and accomplish each.

Finish raising kids.

Finally have relationships down.

When I eliminate all of my flaws.

When I finally save enough money.

Pay enough bills.

Have the right house.

Have things in the right order,

And can begin to enjoy all my dreams uninterrupted.

Or,

is it in the midst of all of these,

And the enjoyment of today and this moment,

REFLECTIONS

With its good and bad mixed in,

And amongst the doubts and flaws,

Mixed with my hopes and dreams,

And the many times I stop and live in the present for a while,

And realize the joy in that,

Before I get wrapped up in the next minute.

Ahhh, that!

Mom

She leads a life of simple goodness,

Caring for others unselfishly,

Enjoying life through her service to others.

Sewing, cooking, cleaning,

Encouraging her family,

Reaching out to those around her in simple ways,

A quilt or a stocking made,

A personal note sent,

Cookies continuously baked and given as gifts,

Enjoying a good meal, book, card game, play, or movie with others,

Engaging in meaningful dialogue,

Growing through her pains,

Always enduring,

Laughing, crying, learning

Her faith with its joys and doubts always present,

Connecting with overlapping groups

In her church, her neighborhood, her circle of family and friends.

Leaving an indelible mark in surprising places

On the young and old alike,

Always learning, reaching, growing, praying;

Every day, leaving life better through her simple, faith-filled actions

And teaching me to be the same.

Memories of Children When they were Young

Singing them to sleep.

Laying on the front yard slope watching the stars.

Putting on their shoes.

Singing Byo My Baby and other songs.

Putting on band-aids.

Singing The Twelve Days Of Christmas in the car.

Going to the grocery to pick out killer desserts.

Having Tootsie Roll Pops lasting contests on trips.

Watching Jaws at the beach.

Making Daddy Specials.

Long Bike rides.

Fifi.

Reading Charlotte's Web.

Thousands more.

Kim

A college degree after years of work;

An accomplishment to be proud of.

But there is so much more:

A youth of learning and happiness,

Giving her parents joy,

A smile of warmth.

Always enjoying what is there.

Whistling and happy –

Pigtails, dolls, sandbox –

Enjoying tasks.

Singing to Juice Newton songs

Simple conversation in her room when I came home from work,

Sleeping with so many stuffed animals and dolls.

Countless questions of wonder.

Watching Andy Griffith with her legs crossed.

Marveling at a new sister

And growing with her as a friend.

Embracing other siblings.

Quietly observing and taking from experiences.

Big, dark eyes

Becoming a young lady.

Growing through awkwardness into a strong woman,

Equally becoming strong as a wife, mother,
worker, friend,

Growing in her surroundings and relationships,

Learning from her mistakes,

Taking joy from everything in life,

From the simple to the complex,

And making a wonderful difference in the world.

Life Realized

I realize life for me through it all —

Marriage,

Raising kids,

Careers,

Friends,

Experiences —

It has all been about helping people,

Trying to slow life down,

Enjoying right now,

And letting go.

Meghan

Quiet, soft and loving;

Freckles on her nose;

Small, simple;

Never complaining.

Experiencing the depth of joy and pain,

Living memories of her grandmother,

Baking cookies.

Gentleness.

Depth of thoughts.

Huge tears at sorrow.

Listening to her talk while walking, and the joy of that;

Seeing me in her and having pride.

Getting simple gifts from her that show she knows me.

Sleeping on the white house floor on the first day, waiting for the furniture.

In my lap with her punctured hand, on the way to the hospital.

Her laugh.

The pride of her own room in order.

Kindness to friends.

Seeking to grow every day.

And gently passing on herself to her children.

Mistakes

Mistakes are things done

On the way to eventually doing the right things

Countless Blessings

The world is beautiful.

Birds sing,

The sky is blue.

Looking forward to experiences is bliss.

Memories are warming.

Giving of myself to others is satisfying.

Financial independence is settling and rewarding.

Patio home living is simple, contented.

Reading gives me peace;

Sitting in my chair with engrossing articles is bliss.

Playing Gin with Anne, joking with her, hearing her life experiences and her hearing mine is enriching.

Sitting in Church on Sundays, believing in God, singing with the choir is peaceful.

Singing in the car is uplifting.

The satisfaction of having made a real difference in the world and continuing to is pleasing.

Feeling Sam & Abby love Papa, watching their thrill and love of small gifts from Mister Red Helm.

Salmon at J Alexander's.

Feeling thin, tan, handsome, healthy –

People smiling at me.

The times I work through my doubts to have glimpses of believing in God.

Great energy with Anne through laughter, loving, watching movies, eating snacks, coffee, muffins and cereal on Saturdays.

Taylor loving me unconditionally, simply, thoroughly from the investment she has made in me.

My work being a living; learning, growing, helping and giving experience

Thinking of more life, starting today.

The times I accept being at peace with whatever is, including the hurt and pain I can't change.

The memories of being a wonderful father, a caring and unconditionally loving spouse, loyal friend, sibling and son.

So appreciative.

Lincoln

My son has a new son.

What an awesome thing!

Tenderness showing in his voice as he tells me;

Humility, pride, thoughtfulness, all at once,

Like silence in church.

And then hearing him tell of the experience –

Big, beautiful child!

Lincoln;

Brown curly hair,

Born a toddler not a baby,

Part of his roots.

Overwhelming happiness and pride.

His voice quiet,

His words confident and sure.

As a grandfather, soothing, warm, happy, silent feelings.

Awesome, reappearing thoughts of Doug's birth and growing up.

Time spent with him and his blessings.

Riding bikes, wild and free.

Handsome,

Passionate,

Sensitive,

Loving,

And now all of that for him to experience with his son.

My faith is strengthened –

What a glorious day!

Nature

Nature blows me away!

A grove of trees on a hill off the highway;

The beautiful sound of flowing water;

Tall grass blowing in a breeze;

Flowers reaching toward the sun;

And everything in balance.

Sam

Grandson,

Godson,

Loving,

Caring,

Kind,

Curious,

Creative.

Three-pointers and falling down and getting fouled.

Quietly learns,

Asks great questions,

Reads,

Grows from the goodness of others.

A person of few words, carefully chosen.

Loyal and protective of family,

Hand in glove with sister Abby,

Growing to the sky to make the world better:

He teaches me!

Sixty

At Sixty I look around at my surroundings:

Plaques, awards, mementos, possessions,

Mostly clutter.

All that matters are relationships built,

People helped,

People who helped me,

The things that last and leave a legacy.

Singing

Singing is exhilarating!

Grabbing a Sinatra tune,

Belting it out,

Closing my eyes and getting lost in the experience,

Totally letting go.

Blending with the orchestra,

Pleasing an appreciative audience:

Time stands still,

Pain doesn't exist,

Perfect blends with orchestra and audience.

An escape like no other.

Swimming

The water glistens as I begin to swim.

I look around at the people in action.

I stretch and put on goggles.

I hesitate and think of a reason not to,

But I jump in the water.

I adjust to the cold and quickly push off the side and start the long process.

I churn through the first few laps;

My energy is high.

I see nature as I come up for air every other stroke;

The sun as it reflects the variety of the world, below and above the water.

I think I can swim forever!

A few laps later, I breathe harder and face my limits, wondering if I can make it to the end.

I struggle and try to talk myself out of continuing:

I am tired today –

No one will know if I stop short!

But I continue,

And a few laps later, I hit my stride and feel a resurgence of my energy –

What a feeling!

I begin to have fresh thoughts,

New ideas,

Better ways of working,

Of living my relationships.

I think of the beach.

I become aware of others swimming and adjust to my own speed –

Not as fast as some, but faster than others.

I countdown the last few laps.

I feel accomplishment;

My energy renews.

I kick hard and feel the satisfaction of making my last lap,

And then, occasionally, kick for one or two more.

I get out of the pool, thrusting myself up the edge.

I walk to the locker room to shower, stretch, change.

I am invigorated and renewed.

I sing Sinatra and think of more ways to enjoy life and be more.

I eat my lunch in the car and ride back to my life –

Alive and Happy!

Sisters and Brothers

An unexpected reward at this point,

To grow in relationship with grown siblings.

We connect more,

Seem to hold hands with each other,

Share memories.

Weekly Zoom calls we look forward to, brought on by COVID,

Inching deeper in thoughts as time passes –

The good and the bad.

Without parents, grandparents, aunts and uncles who were so much to us and now are all gone,

I see the beauty of each of them:

Jane: sensitive, loving, enduring, funny.

John: dedicated, faith-filled, growth through pain, liking solitude, researching, finding new life.

Ted: so kind, thoughtful, realistic, accepting, generous, passionate, creative.

Lucy: so sensitive and caring, kind to the lowest, simple, corporate power flowing through goodness as a person, loyal, giving.

David: curious, ethical, holding to values, youngest, wanting to know siblings better, liking history, appreciating tradition.

So rewarding.

Youth Memories

Some memories stand out from an adolescent life moving at the speed of light:

Getting together for family meals;

Delivering papers and cutting grass;

Smoking cigarettes behind Pookman's Drug Store;

Blue book coin collections;

Nestlé Crunch bars;

1964 Chevy Impala and Topper Motor Scooter;

Top 40 radio and listening to 45s at the record store;

WAKY and WKLO rock and roll stations;

Frisch's and Ranch House drive- ins;

Riding bikes in the neighborhood;

Hot nights going to sleep with a window fan in the summer, in the same room with two brothers;

Neighborhood kick-the-can and street kickball on Cornell Place;

Working as a bag boy at Kroger;

Laughing, talking and exploring with a few friends;
Popsicles after dinner from Pookman's Drug Store;
Memories which are so clear they seem only yesterday;
Molding me and soaring through life with me,
Making me feel always young.

Struggle

Struggle is opportunity,

But not at the particular moment you are having it

Taylor

What it means at this point in my life,

To have a stepdaughter I didn't expect.

Young child,

Growing beautifully,

Someone I sing to,

Laugh with,

Watch swimming,

Diving off of my shoulders.

Someone I say, "What do you think" to, as she asks life's curious questions.

I watch her learn, laugh, fear,

And be near to and learn from her mother,

Becoming her mother.

Following her footsteps in the sand on the beach as she walks.

She stoops to pick up treasures:

I keep both hands full of what she finds.

REFLECTIONS

Some broken shells many would pass by,

She sees as beautiful and gathers.

It is so unexpected, this relationship,

Which I learn and grow from

Much, due to rich experiences learned from three daughters

From past years and similar experiences,

Which give me depth and breadth

And allow me to experience this one with maturity and appreciation.

An experience I didn't expect,

And even resisted, not to be disloyal to wonderful relationships with my daughters;

But this does not diminish that –

It expands it.

And once again, the greatest gems come about unexpected and resisted,

And then relished,

Broadening and enriching my life.

Who will she become?

How will she overcome her fears?

What difference will she make in life?

Who will she make happy, love, learn from, teach?

Growing Pains

The Pain in Life

Gives a deeper ability

To experience joy

Moving Sunrise

There is a part of the road I take each morning to work,

On a clear day,

When I look back over my shoulder,

On a steady rise of the road,

I see the sun come out of the horizon and head to the sky –

Very quickly, as if in fast forward.

And I marvel at that,

As if I had it on a string, like a kite as a child,

And was running forward, pulling:

And the wind takes it up high in the sky.

Eventually I hit a curve in the road and lose sight of the sun,

But the memory is there with me for the day in my mind.

Giving Back

Today, I was invited to meet with a bank customer.

He was at a crossroads and deciding whether or not to sell his very successful business and consult.

I banked Jim, his father and even knew his grandfather.

They had all run the family business in order.

He asked me for my thoughts:

"What would you do in my spot?

What do you think of my plan?"

It helped put in a nutshell what has been satisfying about my career. I am a banker who has helped people!

When I retire, I will remember this day and the people I have banked and helped.

Todd

Youngest child,

Full of energy,

Intrigued by gadgets and all intricate things that move and are connected –

Light switches, computers, television technology –

Wild with energy,

Lover of nature,

Curious,

Recalling memories of loving experiences;

Intensely forgiving and accepting,

A person of passion for life and its adventures

Deeply appreciating family and wanting to grow his own.

Depth easily overlooked in him:

Endless bike rides going where he chooses,

Loving cars for their speed and beauty,

Overcoming all to succeed and be quietly contented.

Adding growth and experience to my life!

Visiting Grandchildren

It is just me and them.

10 to 25 minutes a visit,

Mostly following their lead and listening,

Doing what they ask:

Reading a book to their class,

Throwing the football in the side yard –

"Make me dive for it, Papa!"

Shooting baskets and pretending to be Seth Curry,

Coloring, drawing, reading books in the daycare entrance way,

Walking and balancing on a retaining wall,

Playing rock school on the steps,

Sitting on a tree swing, taking turns pushing,

Looking for small treasures in Papa's convertible –

A mint, a tootsie roll pop, a piece of gum –

"Did Santa come, Papa?"

REFLECTIONS

Picking up from school and walking the Ohio River scenic bridge and talking.

Brown bag lunches in the park by daycare,

Feeding the ducks and throwing rocks into the creek,

Being there with a smile when they wake up from a nap in daycare,

Singing to their class,

Hide and seek on the playground after school.

Such short visits,

But immeasurable joy

And indelible memories!

Elderly Beauty

Simple visits with them when they were old,
Much of their lives lived,
Just relaxing.
No agenda,
Values spilling out,
Sometimes hysterically laughing,
Other times seriousness, tears.
Beaming with pride, love:
Hugs at the end.

Grandma:
In her room,
Reading with a magnifying glass,
Feeling like I'm the only person she loves.
Talking family memories of her parents and siblings,
Asking about my children,

Knitting and sewing materials in her lap,

"How 'bout you, Doug?"

Mom:

Visits after church or midday on a workday,

"Can I get you something?"

Chatting about life:

"What book are YOU reading?"

An occasional ice cream convertible ride –

"You gave me so much to think about!"

Dad:

In his office after I swim,

At a card table on the phone and him stuffing envelopes.

Eating our brown bag lunches.

Giving me thoughts on life and books to read,

Legs comfortably crossed.

His stories of life in AA, Army, growing up, about inspirational readings.

Standing to summarize and say goodbye before hugging and heading down the hall,

Getting back to our routines.

The Most Beautiful Thing

What is the most beautiful thing?

Is it the sun rising and setting and giving us a warmth and glow??

Is it a child being born?

Or a song of deep meaning which pierces the soul?

Or is it grass growing in spring, or leaves of a beautiful color in Fall?

Maybe it's the sounds of a choir or children singing,

Or a meadow deep in a forest with a herd of galloping horses,

Or steady rainfall making glorious noise on a tin roof,

Or hundreds of hot air balloons rising in brilliant color,

Or an orchestra making beautiful sounds,

Or maybe . . .

It is one person being kind to another,

And the beautiful way that can cascade through the world

And lift people's spirits and make them believe in themselves.

THAT is a beautiful Thing!

Wheat Thins and Muenster Cheese

It was always a long few days preparing to teach my college class on Sunday and on Monday during a few breaks at work,

And then teaching the whole three hours of the weekly class on Monday nights.

I was too nervous and involved in preparation to eat all of Monday:

The anticipation in preparation and the passion of lecturing carried me through with a high.

Going home exhausted, I stopped by the grocery and picked up Muenster cheese and wheat thins,

And when I got home, one of the kids who stayed up would climb up on my lap as I ate

And join with me in reaching for the plate full of snacks.

Not many words, but great closeness.

Combining some of life's greatest things:

REFLECTIONS

Loving family,

Teaching others,

Sharing a snack,

Being home.

When I See Myself

When I see myself,

Do I like what I see?

When the music stops,

The confusion stills.

When the world isn't spinning so fast;

When I am alone and it is quiet;

When I am not working or talking or being involved;

When I am finished with the paper;

When the conversation ends,

And I go to bed and cannot sleep,

And it's just me and my thoughts in the darkness,

Going through life,

Facing the gaps,

Measuring what I've accomplished

And what I haven't,

REFLECTIONS

In the solitude:

That is a true test.

Woman in Church

She sits attentively in the front row:

Pious, happy, focused

During mass,

Reverent, faith- filled and inspiring,

My faith grows as I watch her

Bowing, praying and singing along.

Years of loyalty, love, dedication show in her eyes, her smile,

Distant as she is to much of life,

She is in the right place

In the presence of peace in this church full of people.

I have learned from her today,

And I walk away more inspired than I came.

She fulfills the mystery of life for me.

Young Children Singing

This morning I watched as my grandson sang in a youth choir at church:

The happy sounds of youth,

With their simple faith,

All adults giving them constant smiles,

Their moving hands in waving motions,

With beautiful, simple lyrics of life's goodness,

Voices timid individually mold together in a youthful blend,

And overwhelm me,

Touching my heart,

And making me believe in something bigger than all of life.

I watch,

Smile,

Appreciate,

And cry.

Larry

My friend,

Humble and caring,

Quiet and simple,

Touching so many,

Outgoing in leadership for the benefit of others, despite introversion;

Allowing others to see their ordinary goodness,

Never wanting credit,

Living a simple, celibate life without possessions,

Drawn to the most needy in a missionary world –

"You Americans and your gadgets!"

Accepting of me to extreme,

Competing with me for being thin,

Encouraging others,

Dead honest about faults but in a gentle way:

Overcoming all possessions for the sake of loving.

Making a Cake

It was a ritual:

Mom making a cake.

The whirr of the beaters mixing the batter,

Pouring it into the historic cake pans, brown stained from years of baking.

The beaters and bowl are handed fairly to faithfully watching kids for licking.

The oven smell giving rise to an almost completed job.

Warm layers put on upside-down cake pans to cool.

Magic icing preparation begins in a pan over a burner,

Ingredients from memory.

The artist at work, icing the cake in silence:

Top first, then the sides

The completed product put on the counter to wait for dinner

Divvying up the utensils and pan again to waiting children,

Leaving enough icing on each to be worth the licking reward –

Every child getting a fair share.

On birthdays, candles taking their place on the top of the cake,

And the birthday child picks the type of cake and icing –

Mom always the cake cutter,

Slicing in sizes that leave enough for at least one more meal:

More than a cake baked.

Tradition.

Smiles.

Love.

Memories.

Gifts from Children

A handmade macramé leather belt of flags.

Papa's Mouse Pad with grandson pictures.

A hat from a college visit or a honeymoon.

A model of my car from a trip to Germany.

Best Dad Ever coffee cup.

A matching car-color travel mug.

A cardinal paperweight

Assorted ties.

Handmade Father's Day and birthday cards with artwork.

A Rumi book of quotes.

All worn thin, discolored or stained,

Long forgotten they were given by the child,

But forever cherished,

Sitting on a desk, a dresser or a nightstand –

The giver of every gift known,

Memories of being loved,

Never thrown away,

Always worn, displayed,

And feeling special to have received.

Louisville Orchestra Pops

I have been going to Pops concerts with the Louisville Orchestra for over 25 years for a couple of reasons: because I love the Louisville Orchestra; and I love to watch them blend with Pop artists to make both better.

When I went to a concert this past Saturday night, which featured the Beach Boys, many things were the same as always: the talented, passionate beauty of the orchestra, the nostalgia of a great pops group and the loyal patrons who have been coming, like me, for over 25 years.

But a few things were different: A sellout crowd for the third time this season because of youthful, new patrons; a group of three people in their 20s standing, clapping and dancing until they made others do so; a father with a young son in the balcony swaying back and forth; hundreds coming for maybe their first experience of the Louisville Orchestra!

I was so pleased for the loyalty of longtime patrons, to see new patrons swelling the crowd. And for the future of the Louisville Orchestra and its continuing legacy.

Beach Vacation

I encountered all of life at the beach.

I watched a golden sunrise from the beginning.

I pondered my faith, gazing at the sea.

I loved and reminisced with my wife.

I shared meals full of laughter and stories with family.

I held a grandson and answered his questions.

I walked the shore with three generations and experienced the quickness of the movement of life.

I watched a beautiful sunset until the end.

Turning Seventy

Who would think I would reach 70 so fast?
Feeling still young, passionate, alive –
Feeling middle-aged, not old!
Almost forgetting I ever had a banking career,
Lots of awards,
Teaching others as a professor.
Life going fast and slow at the same time:
I think more, slow down, enjoy books,
Read a lot, but only what I like,
Surprisingly and humbly still learning each day,
Even through pain and the wildly unexpected,
Both good and bad.

Teets Court

A basketball court in our yard growing up,

Where a torn-down garage once was,

For two brothers who loved basketball.

Built from money left by a cousin Teets in a will, to my brother who was her Godson –

Otherwise unaffordable.

Unexpected gift;

Years of playing with each other and with friends,

Getting lost in imagination,

Creating memories,

Bad weather never preventing games,

Dribbling a wet ball during rain,

Playing through cold and snowfalls,

Lighting up at night with the porchlight,

Tilting the radio in a back porch window and adding music.

Playing every day,

Bragging-rights games with friends,

Better than Madison Square Garden,

Proudly writing Teets Court in wet concrete for lifetime naming rights.

Riding the Bus

Two small children, one car and a small salary:

A transfer to the downtown office presented challenges.

Number 15 Jeffersontown Transit Express was
the solution.

35 cents a ride,

No paying downtown to park.

The one family car stayed at home for emergency use.

All bus riders were strangers at first,

But they became people I nodded to,

Then got to know,

Then became friends with.

The same driver every day.

Birthdays were celebrated with cakes.

Dozens of hellos walking down the aisle.

Stories were told,

Books were read,

REFLECTIONS

Rain or shine I walked to the bus stop and waited every day.

If someone didn't get on at their stop, we wondered why.

A sacrifice became a ritual enjoyed.

Relaxing trips and great memories.

Looking Around

I can look almost in any direction any day and have a blazing smile and satisfaction.

Nature, faith, friends, accomplishments –

Just life.

But periods of lack of this connection pierce me and I have to relax and accept my way through them.

Peace comes from not blaming anybody or anything.

Untitled Quote

Everything is a love story

January Thoughts

What will I do differently this year?

Let's just see.

Ask myself this every year.

Illusions

Just because they smile at you doesn't mean they like you,

But just because they don't smile at you doesn't mean they don't like you.

Immaterial what others think of me:

Only what I think of me.

Conclusion

It has been a labor of love sharing these reflections.

Writing each one at the time was special.

But seeing them as a collective work and the process of putting them together in this book has added a new dimension.

Everyone's life, even the simple ones like mine, matters a great deal and has an impact on the world, like a pebble thrown in a pond and the ripples it creates.

This book has exceeded my goal of leaving a legacy to those people important in my life and has helped me appreciate them even more.

For others who may read this, I hope my experiences will have brought to life similar experiences for you or for people you love.

I hope it will give you at least one opportunity to share your appreciation with some special person in your life.

Thanks,
Doug Helm

"And in the end
The love you take
Is equal to the love you make."

From "The End"
A song by the Beatles

The End

About the Author

Doug Helm grew up in Louisville, Kentucky where he lives with his wife, Anne.

After a career in commercial banking with several regional and national banks, Doug enjoys a second career with MCM CPAs & Advisors, a regional CPA and Consulting firm where he leads the firm's sales efforts and consults with business clients, helping them with their banking relationships and borrowing needs.

He received undergraduate and graduate degrees from Bellarmine University and is also a graduate of Stonier Graduate School of Banking.

He has taught commercial lending and money & banking courses at Bellarmine University as part of a bank continuing education program. He has also taught commercial banking and thesis advisory courses at Stonier Graduate Banking at Rutgers University and at the University of Delaware.

He has served on the Louisville Orchestra and Stonier Graduate Banking School boards and currently serves on the Junior Achievement of Kentuckiana board.

For fun, Doug enjoys spending time with family and friends, reading, singing, swimming, traveling and following University of Louisville sports.

He has produced two musical CDs: Doug Sings Frank & Doug Helm Home For Christmas.

>Doug can be reached at:
reflectionsbydoughelm@gmail.com

www.ingramcontent.com/pod-product-compliance
Lightning Source LLC
Chambersburg PA
CBHW071459070526
44578CB00001B/389